Penguin & Tiny Shrimp
DON'T DO
BeDTime!

words by
Cate Berry

pictures by
Charles Santoso

BALZER + BRAY
An Imprint of HarperCollins Publishers

Balzer + Bray is an imprint of HarperCollins Publishers.

Penguin and Tiny Shrimp Don't Do Bedtime!
Text copyright © 2018 by Cate Berry
Illustrations copyright © 2018 by Charles Santoso
All rights reserved. Manufactured in China.
No part of this book may be used or reproduced in any manner whatsoever without written
permission except in the case of brief quotations embodied in critical articles and reviews.
For information address HarperCollins Children's Books, a division of HarperCollins Publishers,
195 Broadway, New York, NY 10007.
www.harpercollinschildrens.com

ISBN 978-0-06-249153-4

The artist digitally created the illustrations for this book.
Typography by Aurora Parlagreco
18 19 20 21 22   SCP   10 9 8 7 6 5 4 3 2 1
❖
First Edition

For David, Milo, and Annabelle Pearl —C.B.

For Emily —C.S.

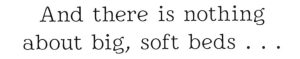

And there is nothing about big, soft beds . . .

No!

Or cozy covers . . .

No!

Or super-squishy pillows . . .

Ohhhhhh, squishy pillows.

One thing this book will
never do is make you tired.

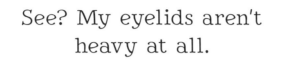